PIANO • VOCAL • GUITAR

KELLY CLARKSON

BREAKAWAY

ISBN 0-634-09824-1

HAL•LEONARD®
CORPORATION
7777 W. BLUEMOUND RD. P.O. BOX 13819 MILWAUKEE, WI 53213

Visit Hal Leonard Online at
www.halleonard.com

CONTENTS

BREAKAWAY

Words and Music by BRIDGET BENENATE,
AVRIL LAVIGNE and MATTHEW GERRARD

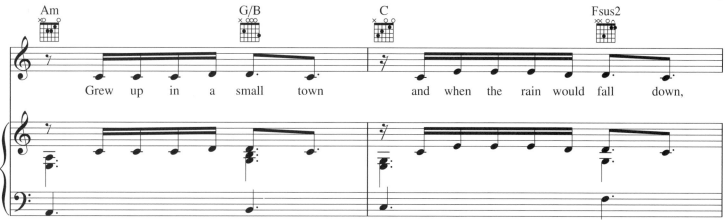

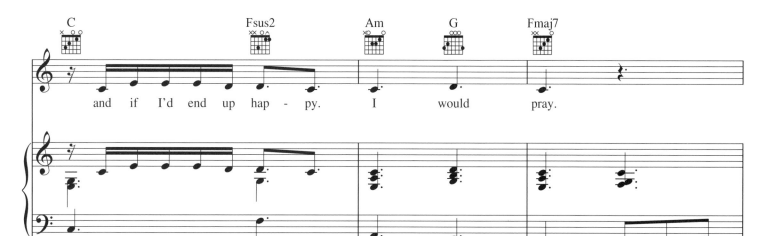

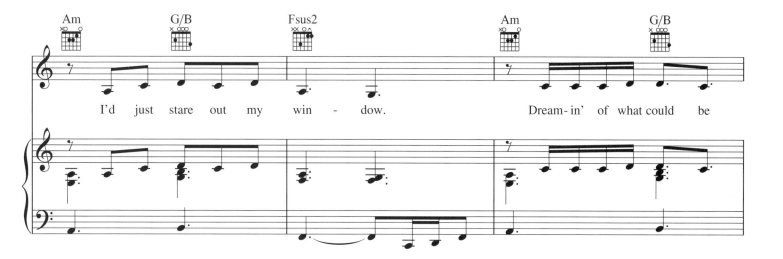

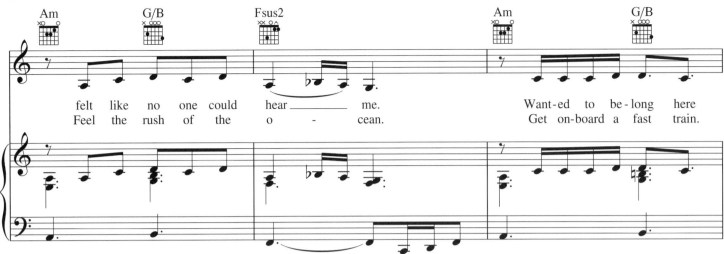

felt like no one could hear _____ me. Want-ed to be-long here
Feel the rush of the o - cean. Get on-board a fast train.

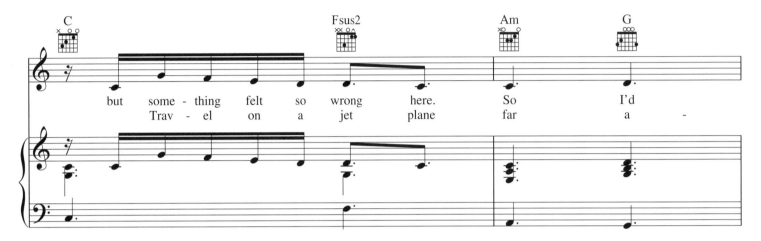

but some-thing felt so wrong here. So I'd
Trav - el on a jet plane. So far a -

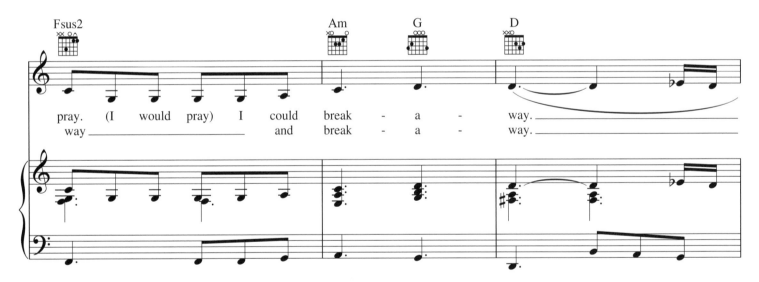

pray. (I would pray) I could break - a - way. _____
way _____ and break - a - way. _____

_____ } I'll spread my wings and I'll learn how to fly. _____ I'll

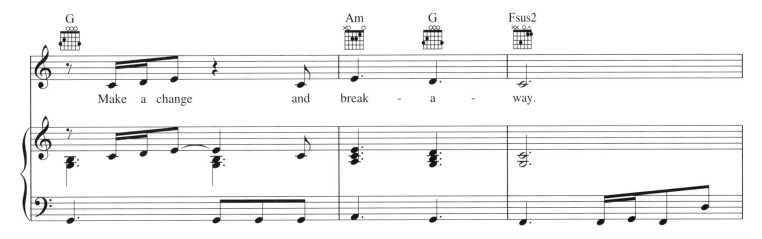

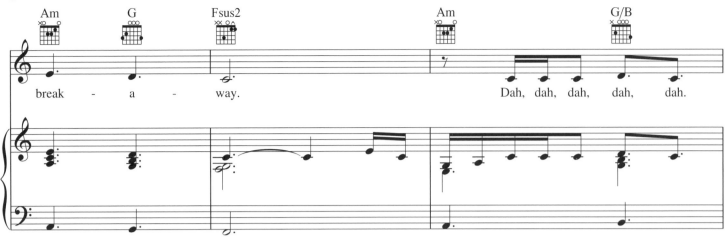

break - a - way. Dah, dah, dah, dah, dah.

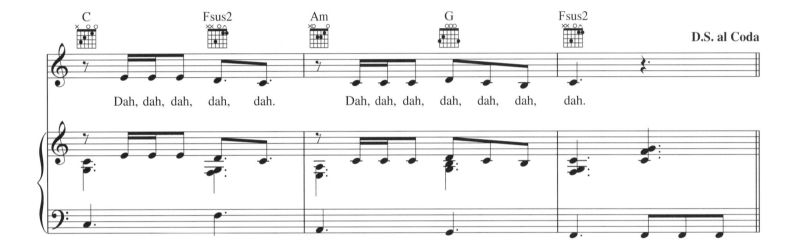

Dah, dah, dah, dah, dah. Dah, dah, dah, dah, dah, dah, dah.

D.S. al Coda

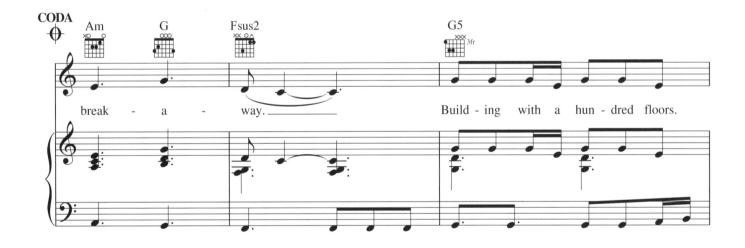

CODA

break - a - way. _____ Build - ing with a hun - dred floors.

Swing-ing 'round re-volv-ing doors. May-be I don't know where they'll take _____ me. But,

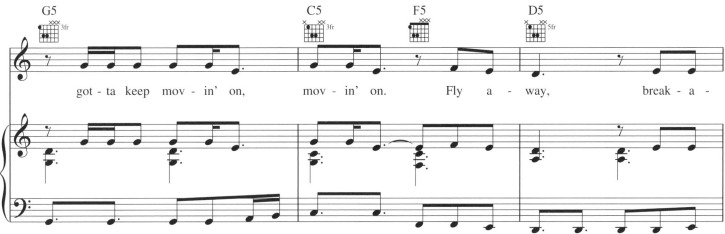

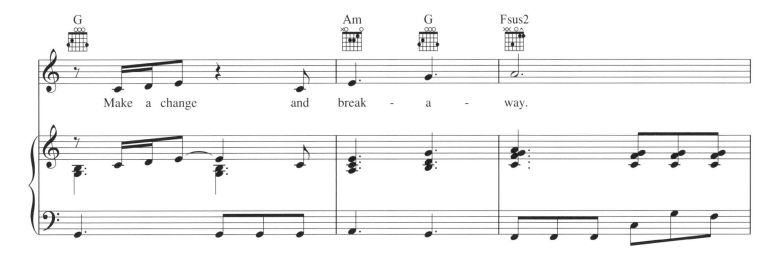

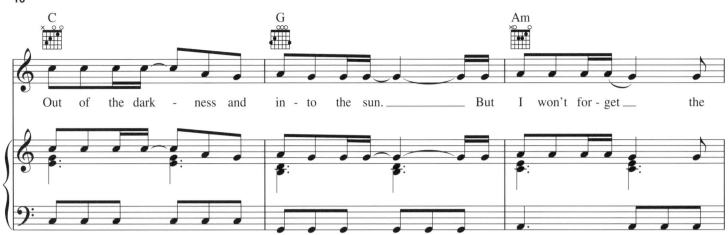

Out of the dark - ness and in - to the sun._____ But I won't for-get ___ the

place I come from. I got-ta take a risk. Take a chance. Make a change and

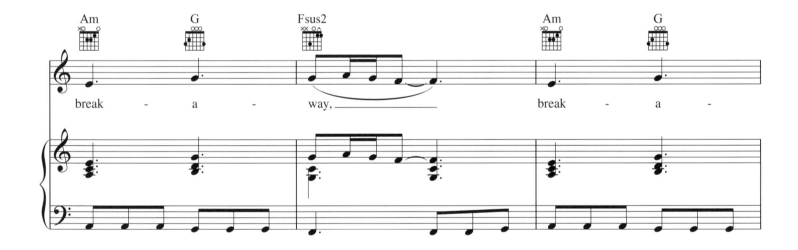

break - a - way, _____ break - a -

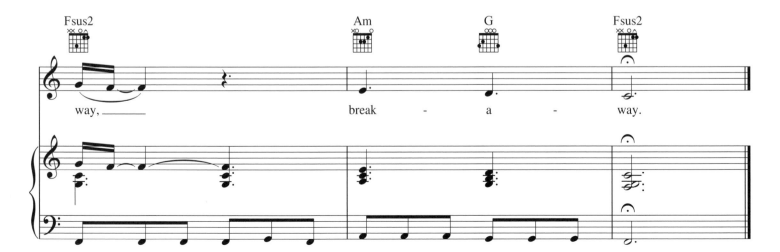

way, _____ break - a - way.

SINCE U BEEN GONE

Words and Music by MARTIN SANDBERG
and LUKASZ GOTTWALD

Moderately fast

Here's the thing: we
You ded - i - cat - ed, you
How can I put it? You

start - ed out friends.
took the time.
put me on.

It was cool, but it was all pre - tend.
Was - n't long 'til I called you mine.
I e - ven fell for that stu - pid love song.

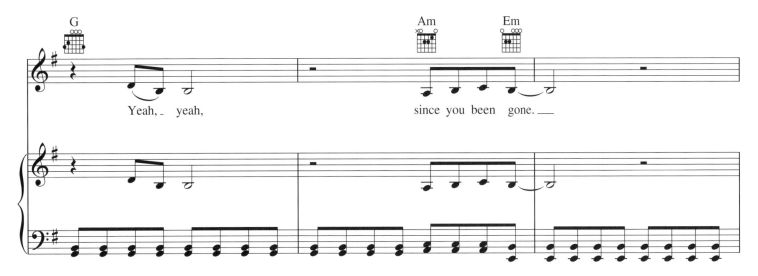

Yeah, yeah, since you been gone.

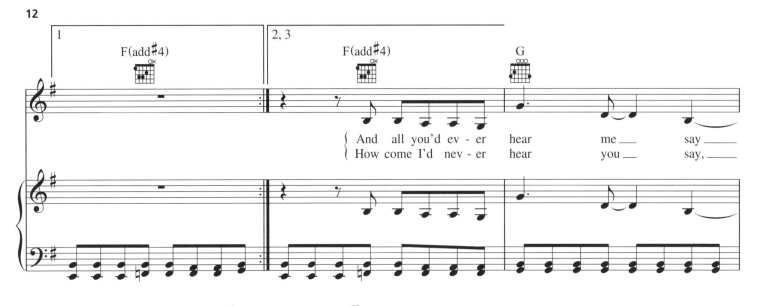

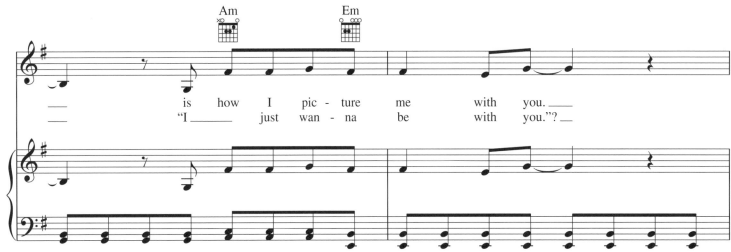

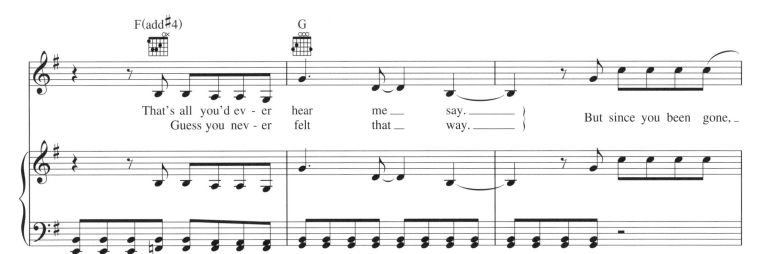

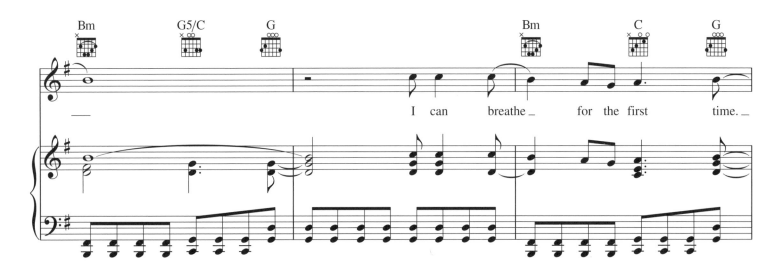

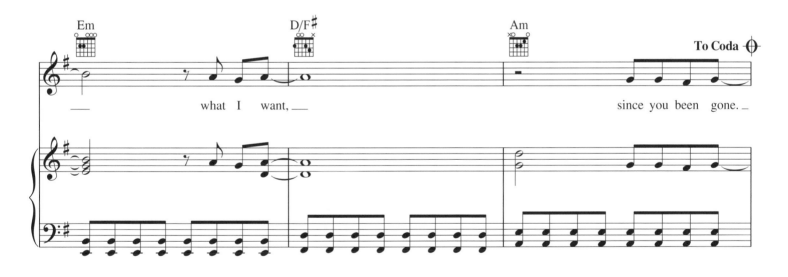

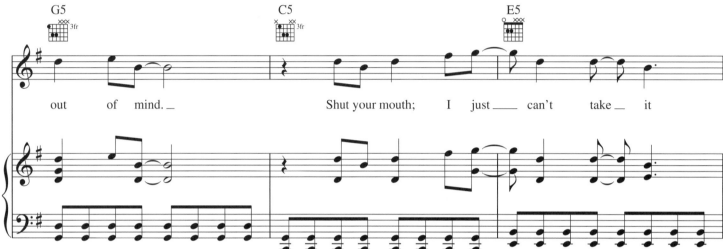

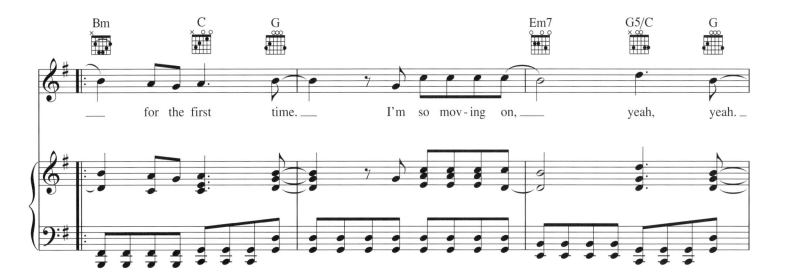

Since you been gone, ___ I can breathe ___ for the first time. ___ I'm so mov-ing on, ___ yeah, yeah. ___

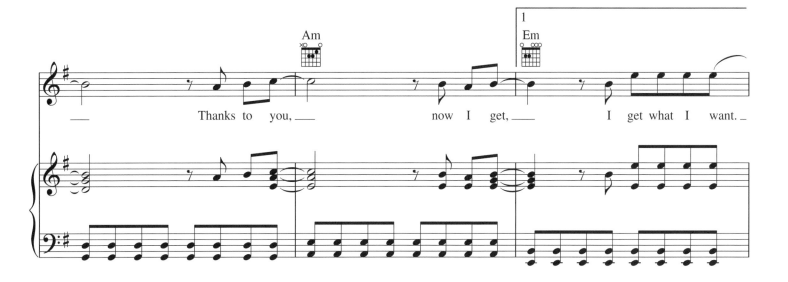

Thanks to you, ___ now I get, ___ I get what I want. ___

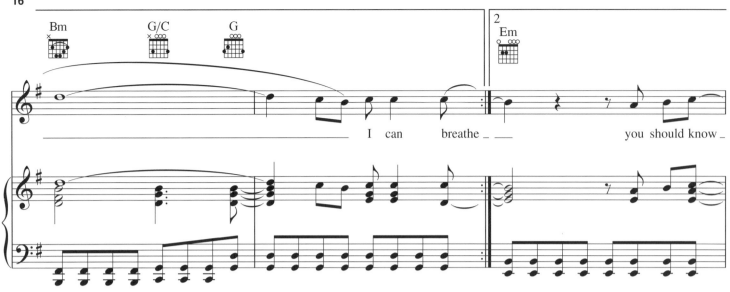

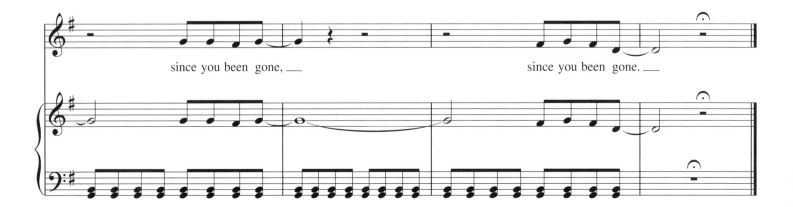

BEHIND THESE HAZEL EYES

Words and Music by KELLY CLARKSON,
MARTIN SANDBERG and LUKASZ GOTTWALD

ev - 'ry-thing, it felt __ so right, _____ un - break - a - ble, __ like
is what I pre - tend __ to be: _____ so to - geth - er, but __ so

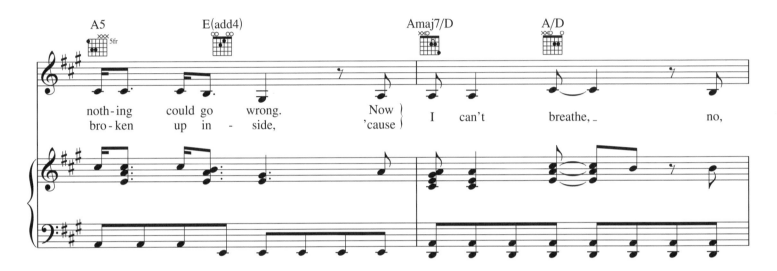

noth-ing could go wrong. Now 'cause } I can't breathe, __ no,
bro - ken up in - side,

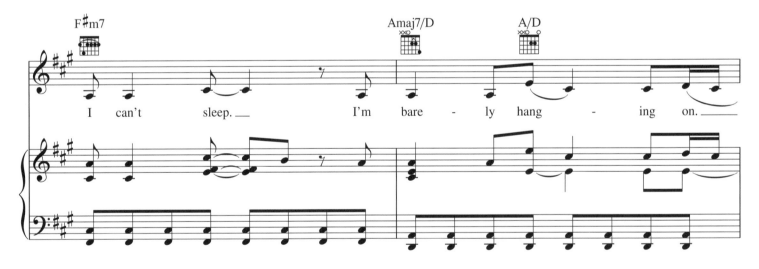

I can't sleep. __ I'm bare - ly hang - ing on. __

Here I am __ once a - gain. __ I'm

torn in - to piec - es, can't de - ny ___ it, can't pre - tend. ___ Just

thought you were the one. ___ Bro - ken up ___ deep in - side, ___ but

you won't get to see ___ the tears ___ I cry ___ be -

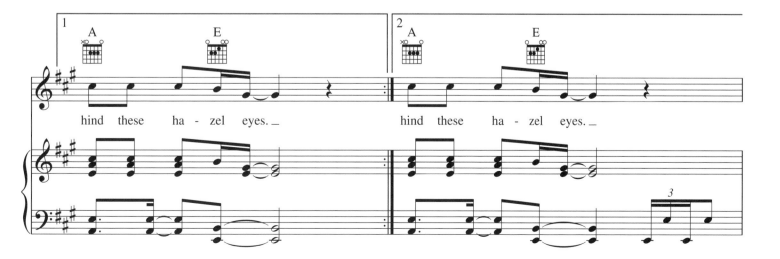

hind these ha - zel eyes. ___   hind these ha - zel eyes. ___

20

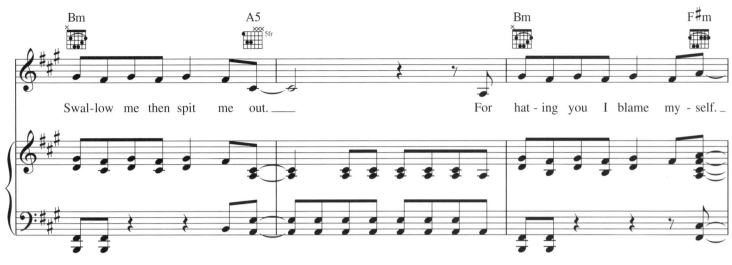

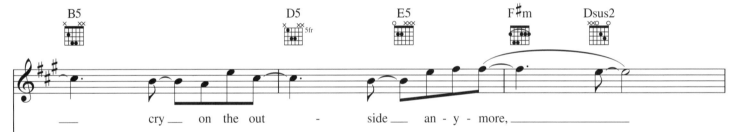

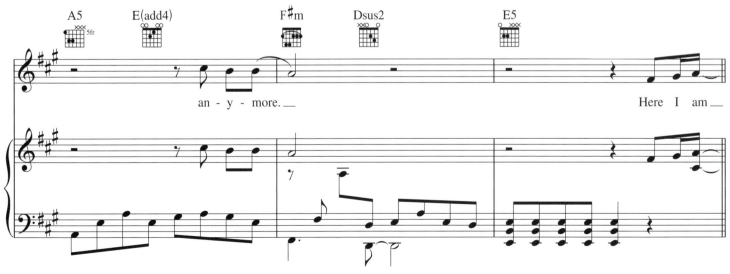

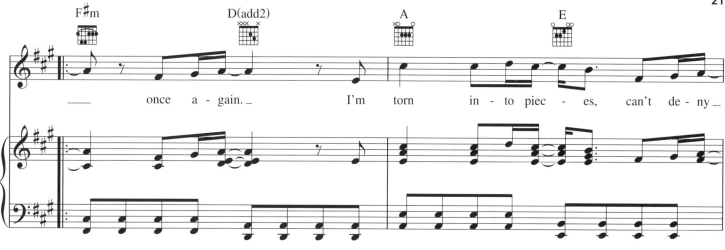

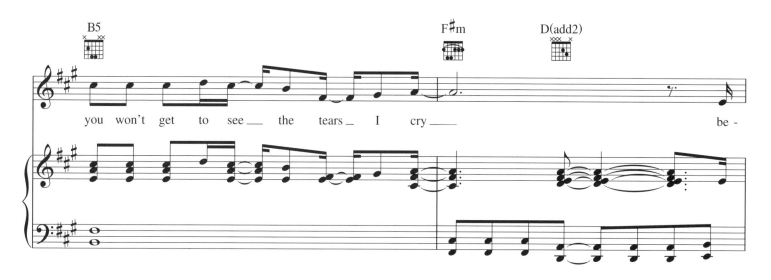

BECAUSE OF YOU

Words and Music by KELLY CLARKSON,
BEN MOODY and DAVID HODGES

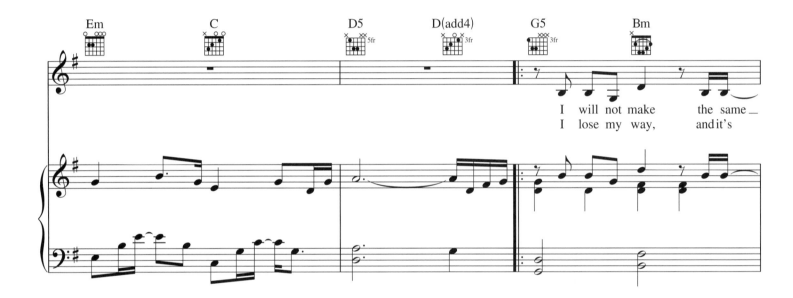

I will not make _____ the same _____
I lose my way, _____ and it's

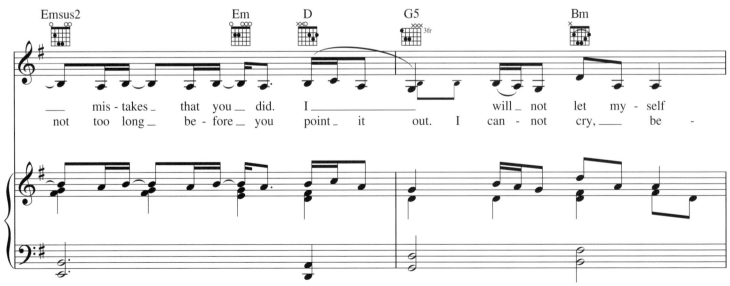

_____ mis - takes _____ that you _____ did. I _____ will _____ not let my - self
not too long _____ be - fore _____ you point _____ it out. I can - not cry, _____ be -

* Recorded a half step higher.

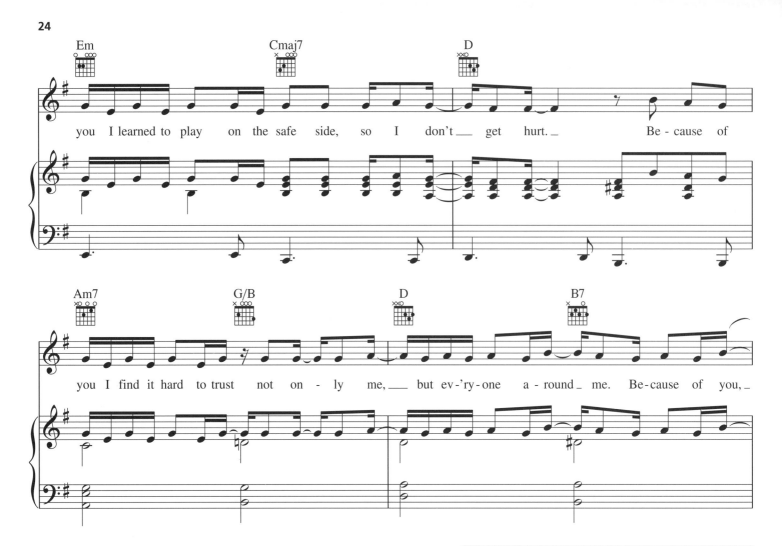

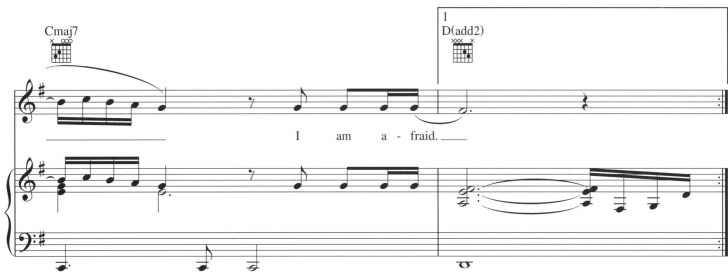

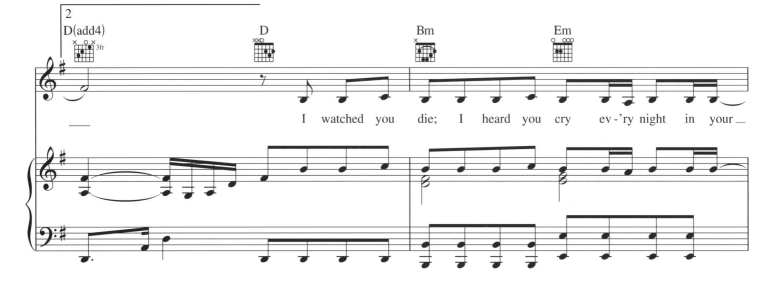

sleep. ____ I was so young; you should have known bet-ter than to lean ____

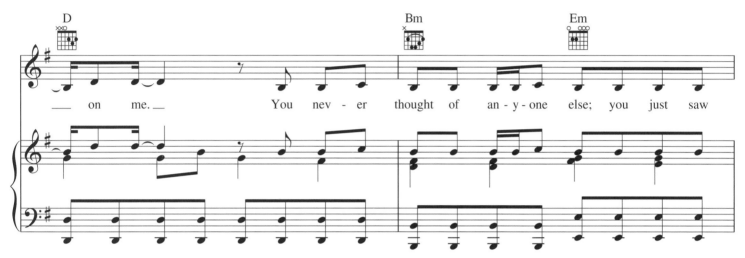

____ on me. ____ You nev - er thought of an - y - one else; you just saw

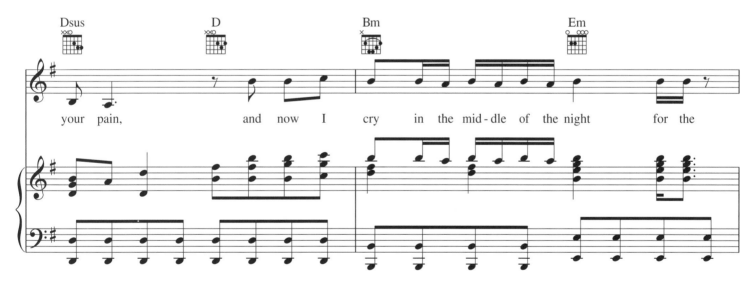

your pain, and now I cry in the mid - dle of the night for the

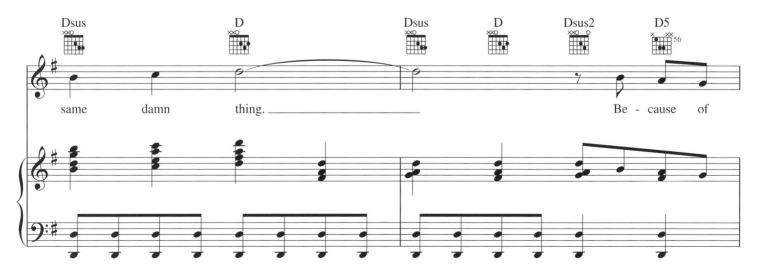

same damn thing. _____ Be - cause of

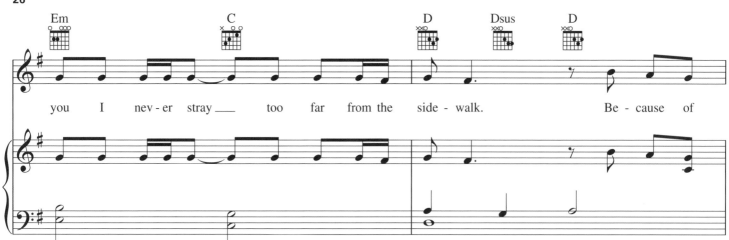

you I nev-er stray ___ too far from the side-walk. Be-cause of

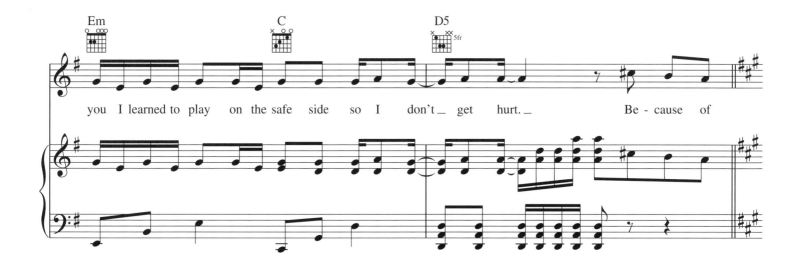

you I learned to play on the safe side so I don't ___ get hurt. ___ Be-cause of

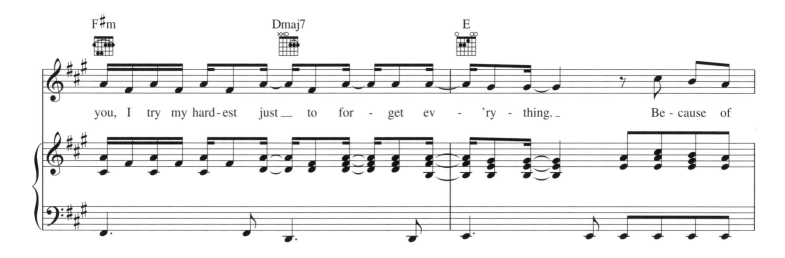

you, I try my hard-est just ___ to for-get ev-'ry-thing. ___ Be-cause of

you, I don't know how to let an-y-one else ___ in. ___ Be-cause of you, ___

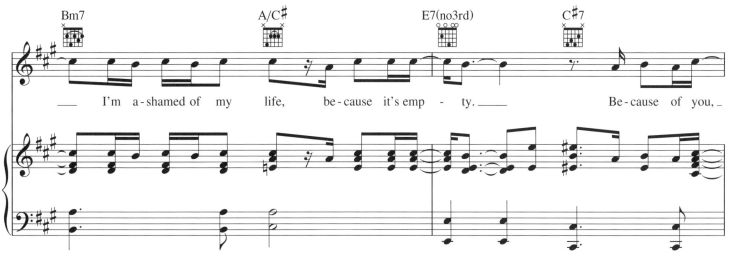

I'm a-shamed of my life, be-cause it's emp - ty. ____ Be-cause of you, ____

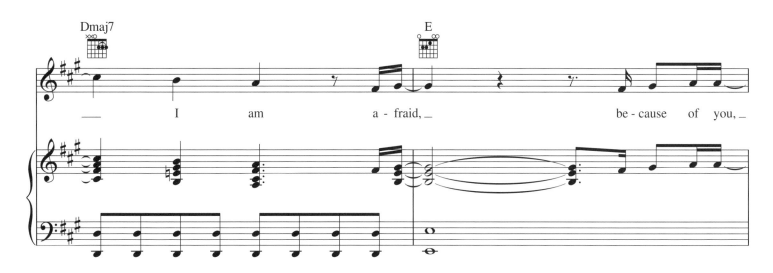

____ I am a - fraid, __ be - cause of you, __

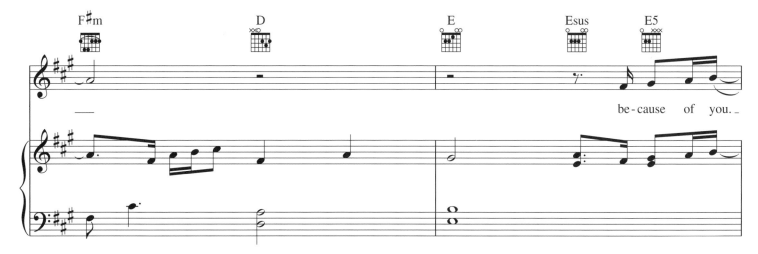

be - cause of you. __

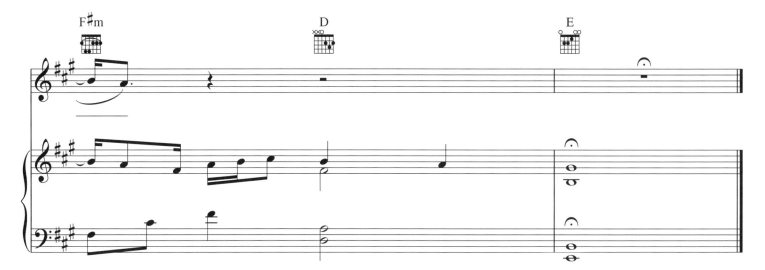

GONE

Words and Music by JOHN SHANKS
and KARA DioGUARDI

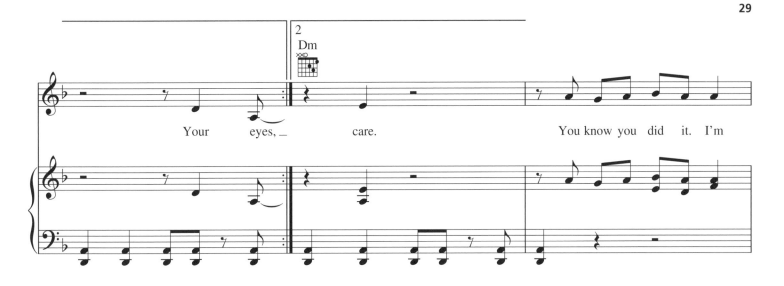

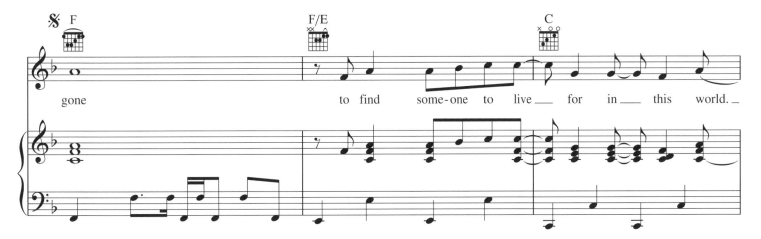

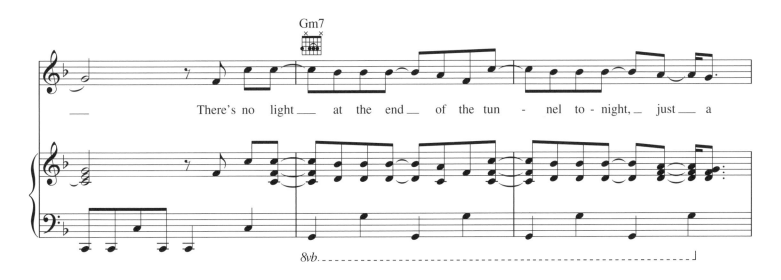

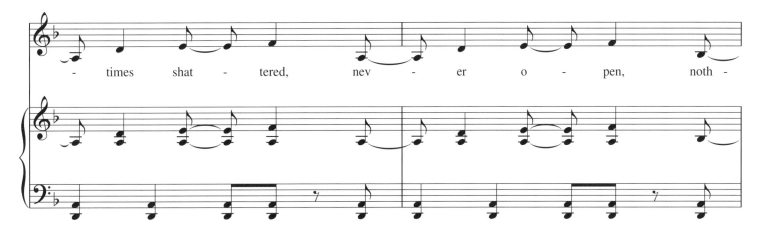

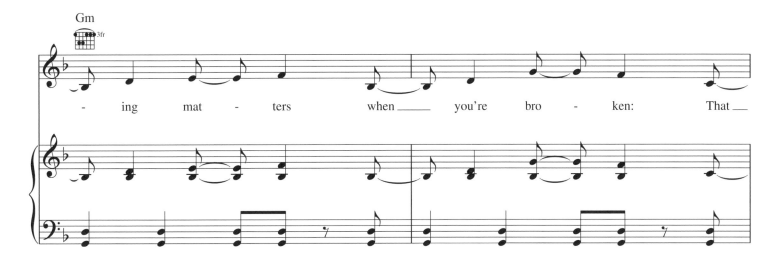

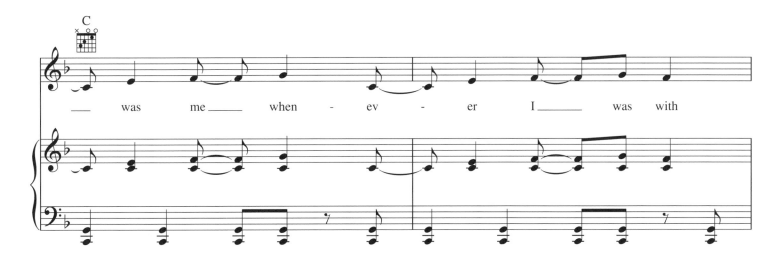

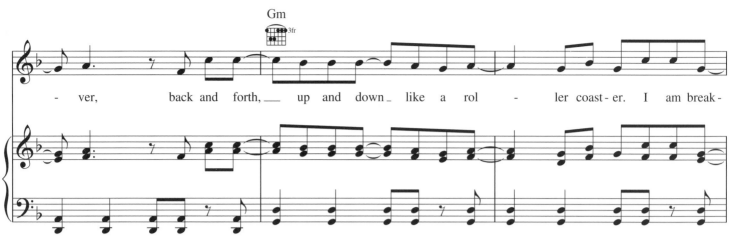

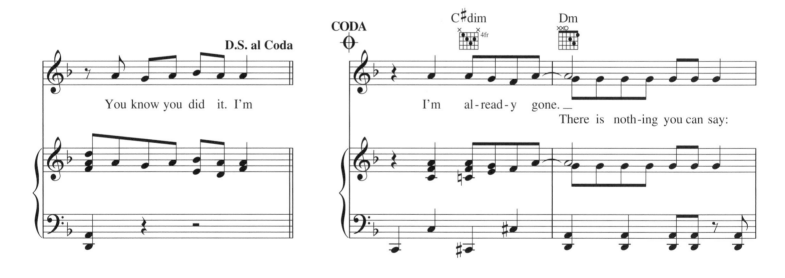

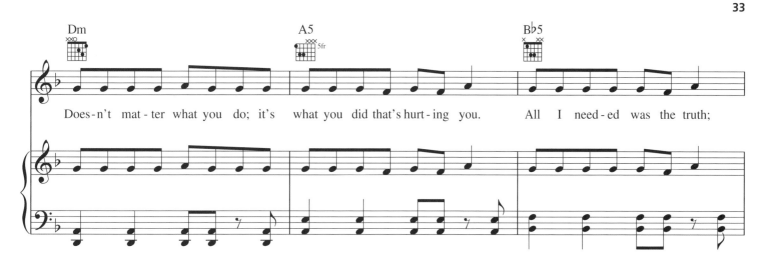

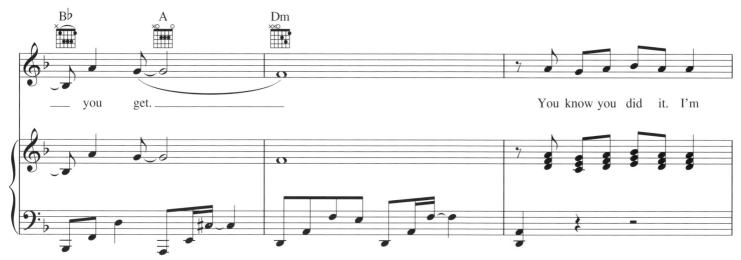

gone   to find some-one to live ___ for in ___ this world. ___

___ There's no light ___ at the end ___ of the tun - nel to-night, ___ just ___ a

bridge that I got-ta burn. ___   You are wrong ___

if you think you can walk ___ right through ___ my door. ___

That is just __ so you, __ com-ing back __ when I've fi - nal - ly moved. __

on. ___ I'm al - read - y gone. ___ *Lead vocal ad lib.*

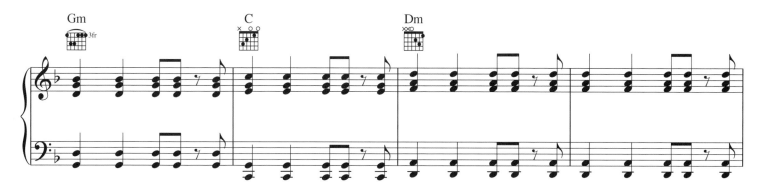

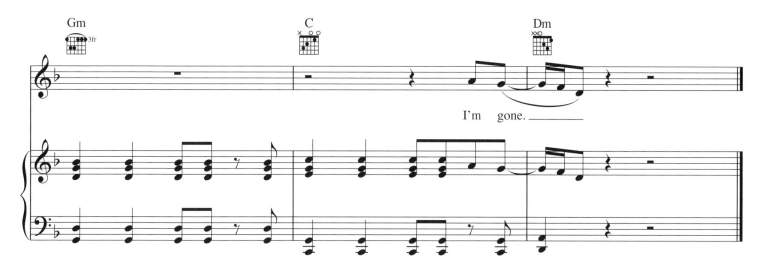

I'm gone. _____

ADDICTED

Words and Music by KELLY CLARKSON,
BEN MOODY and DAVID HODGES

* *Recorded a half step lower.*

dict - ed to you. ___ It's like I can't think ___ with - out you

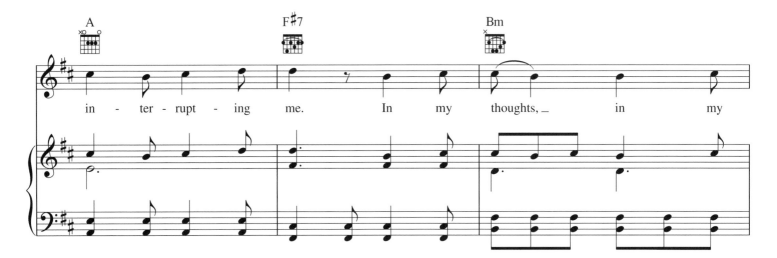

in - ter - rupt - ing me. In my thoughts, ___ in my

dreams, ___ you've tak - en o - ver me. ___ It's like I'm not

me. ___ It's like I'm not me. ___ It's like I'm

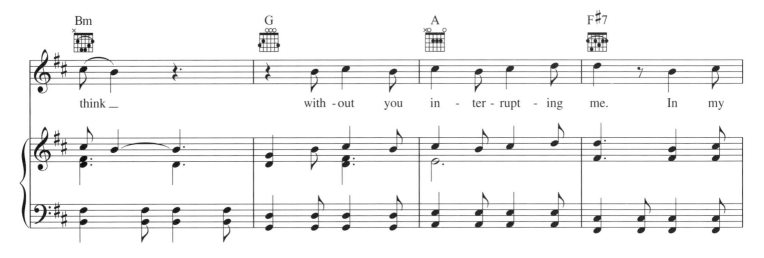

WHERE IS YOUR HEART

Words and Music by KELLY CLARKSON,
CHANTAL KREVIAZUK and KARA DioGUARDI

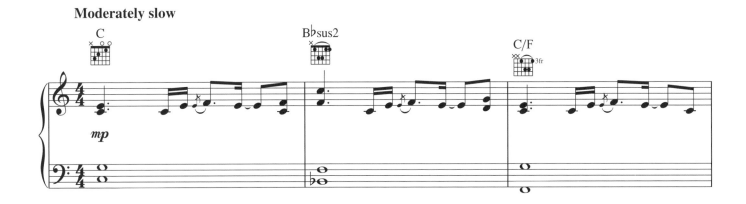

I don't be - lieve _____ in the

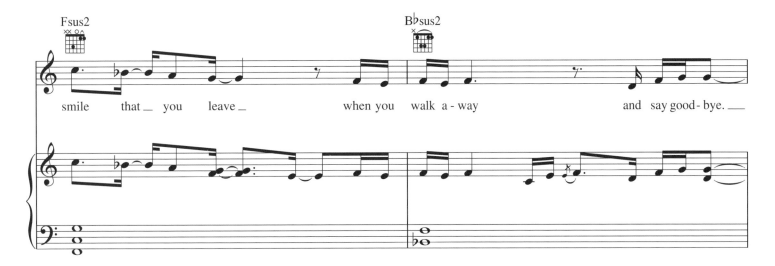

smile that _ you leave _ when you walk a - way and say good- bye. _

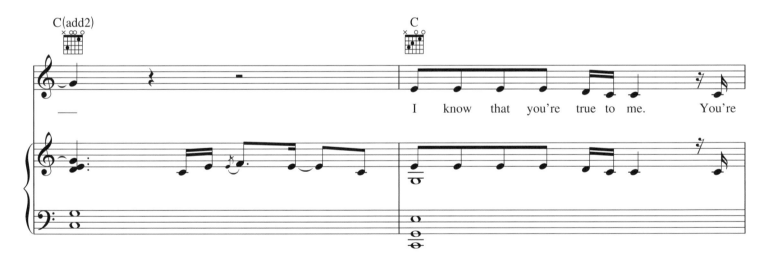

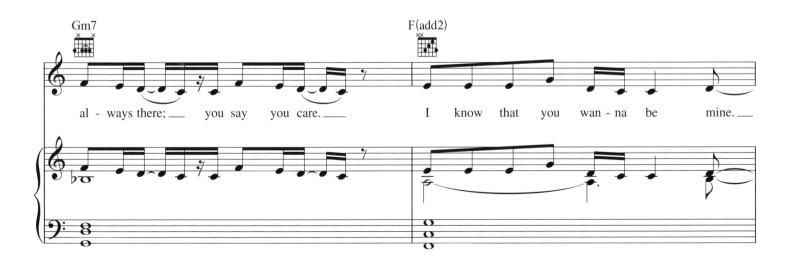

where is your ___ heart? _____ I don't un - der - stand. ___

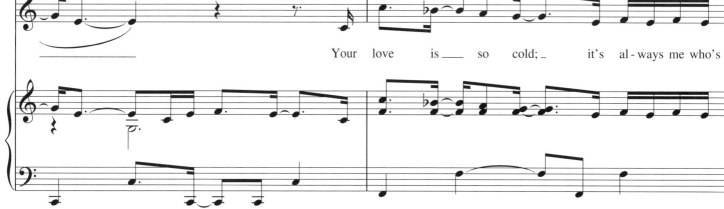

_____ Your love is ___ so cold; _ it's al - ways me who's

reach-ing out for your hand. _____ And I've ___ al - ways

dreamed _____ that love would_ be ef - fort-less, like a

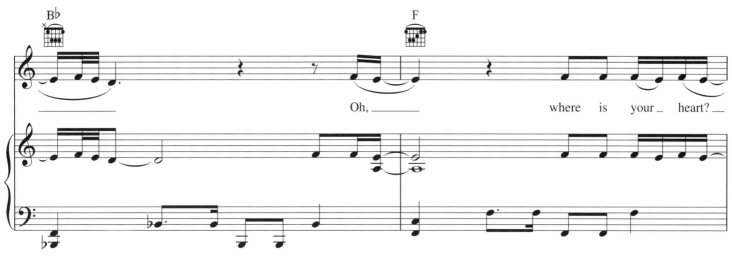

Oh, _____ where is your _ heart? __

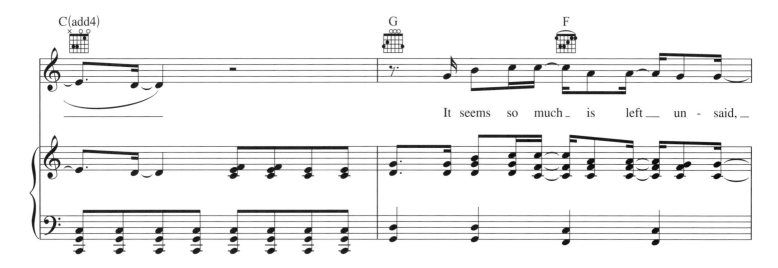

It seems so much _ is left _ un - said, _

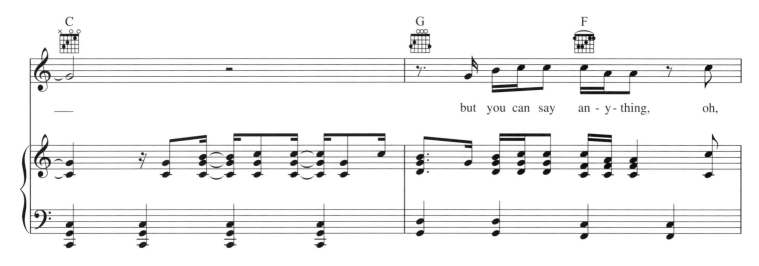

but you can say an - y - thing, oh,

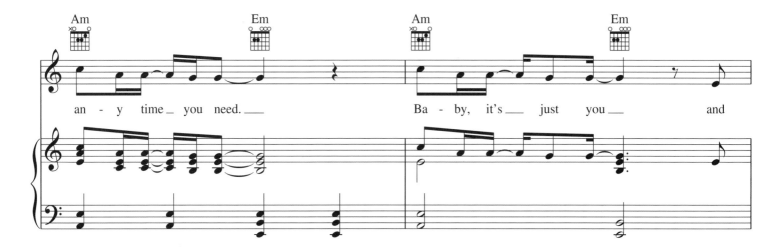

an - y time _ you need. __ Ba - by, it's _ just you _ and

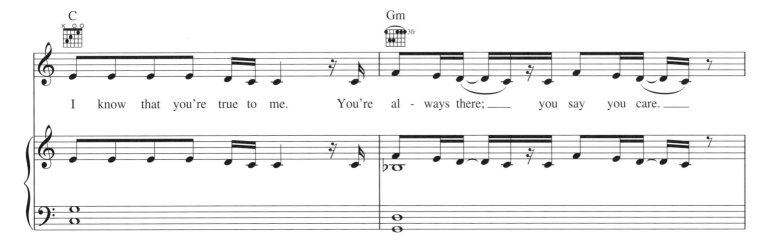

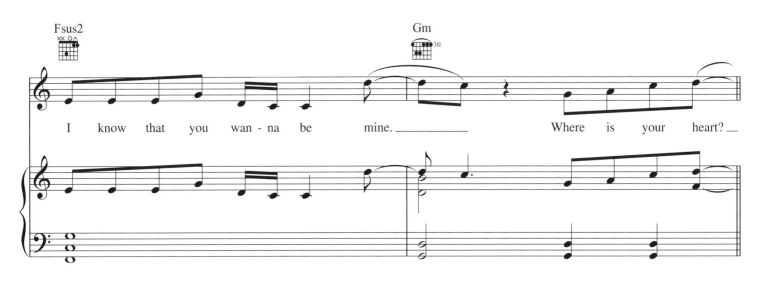

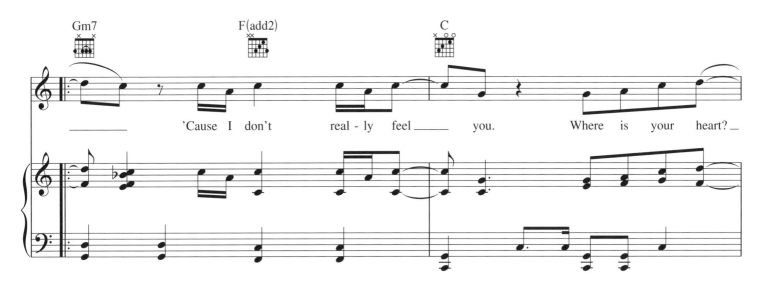

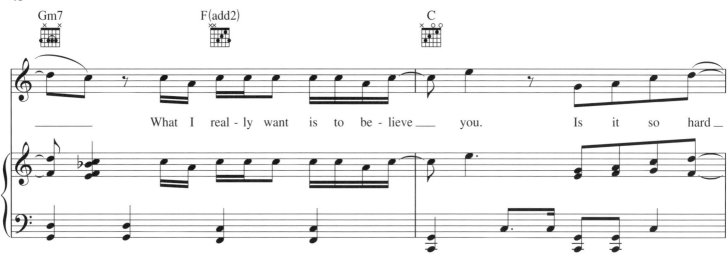

What I real-ly want is to be-lieve ___ you. Is it so hard ___

to give me what I need? I want your heart to bleed, _ and that's all ___ I'm ask - ing for. _

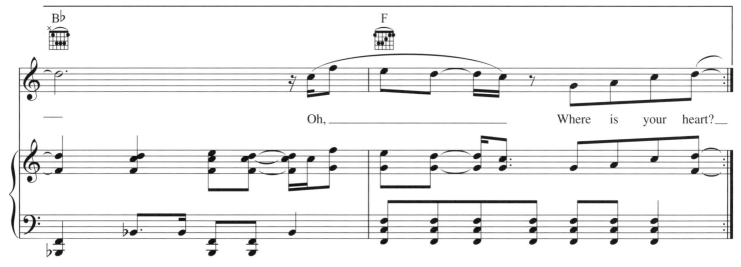

Oh, _____ Where is your heart? ___

heart to bleed, _ and that's all ___ I'm ask - ing for. _____

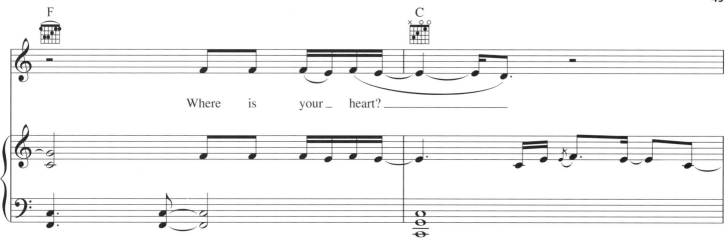

Where is your ___ heart? _____

Where is your ___ heart? _____

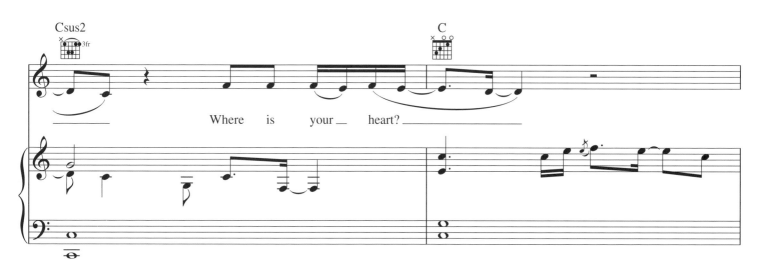

_____ Where is your ___ heart? _____

Where is ___ your ___ heart? _____

WALK AWAY

Words and Music by KELLY CLARKSON, CHANTAL KREVIAZUK,
RAINE MAIDA and KARA DioGUARDI

Moderately fast

You've got your moth - er and your
I've wait - ed here for you like

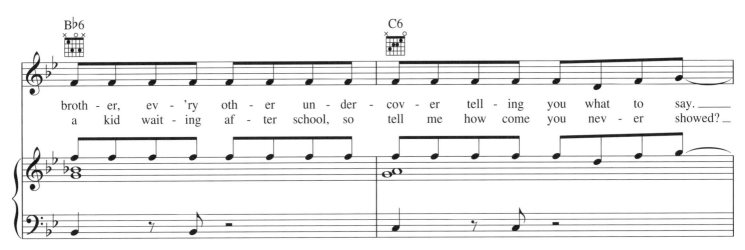

broth - er, ev - 'ry oth - er un - der - cov - er tell - ing you what to say. ___
a kid wait - ing af - ter school, so tell me how come you nev - er showed? ___

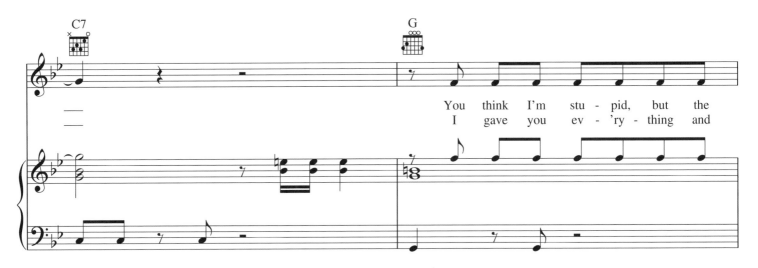

___ You think I'm stu - pid, but the
___ I gave you ev - 'ry - thing and

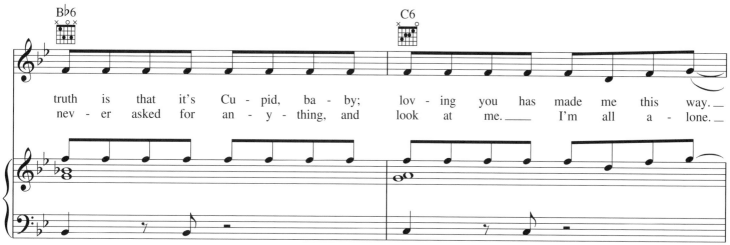

truth is that it's Cu - pid, ba - by; lov - ing you has made me this way. __
nev - er asked for an - y - thing, and look at me. __ I'm all a - lone. __

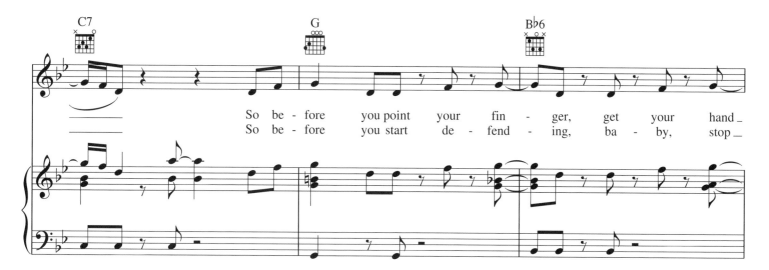

__ So be - fore you point your fin - ger, get your hand __
__ So be - fore you start de - fend - ing, ba - by, stop __

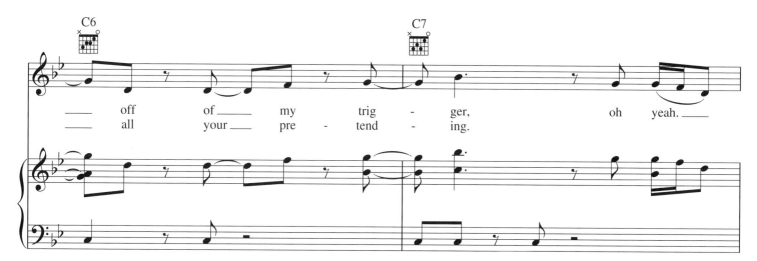

__ off of __ my trig - ger, oh yeah. __
__ all your __ pre - tend - ing.

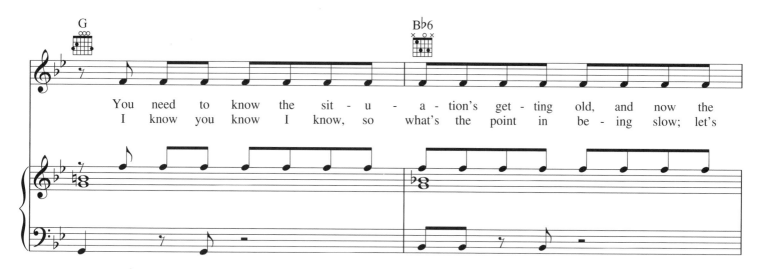

You need to know the sit - u - a - tion's get - ting old, and now the
I know you know I know, so what's the point in be - ing slow; let's

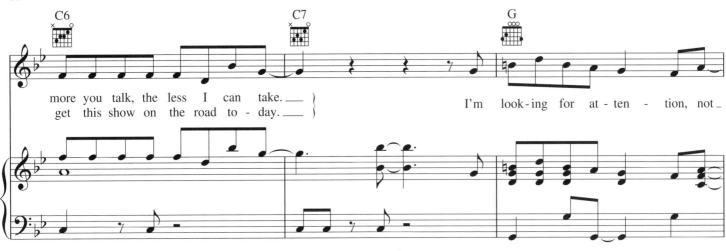

more you talk, the less I can take. ___
get this show on the road to-day. ___

I'm look-ing for at-ten-tion, not ___

___ an-oth-er ques-tion, should ___ you stay or should you go?

Well, if

you don't have the an-swer, why ___ you still ___ stand-ing here?

Hey, hey, hey, hey, ___

___ just walk a-way.

(Just walk a-way.) ___

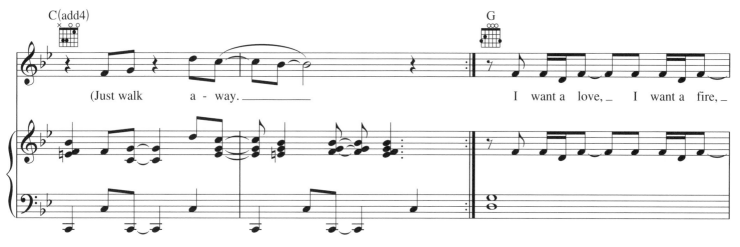

(Just walk a - way. _____

I want a love, _ I want a fire, _

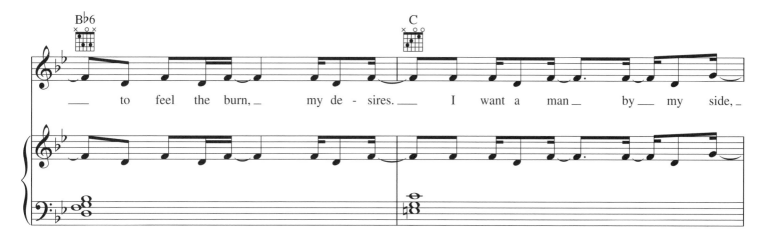

____ to feel the burn, _ my de - sires. ____ I want a man _ by _ my side, _

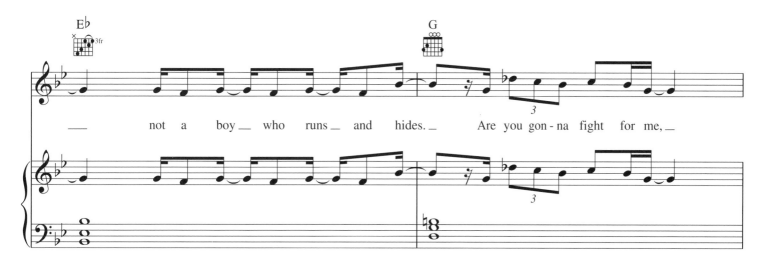

____ not a boy _ who runs _ and hides. ____ Are you gon - na fight for me, _

die for me, live _ and breathe _ for me? ____ Do you care _ for me, _ 'cause

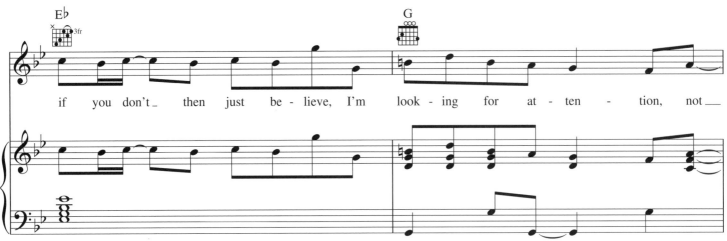

if you don't_ then just be - lieve, I'm look - ing for at - ten - tion, not_

_ an - oth - er ques - tion, should_ you stay or should you go? Well, if

you don't have the an - swer, why_____ you still_____ stand - ing here?

8vb

Hey, hey, hey, hey,_____ just walk a - way. If you don't have the an - swer,_____

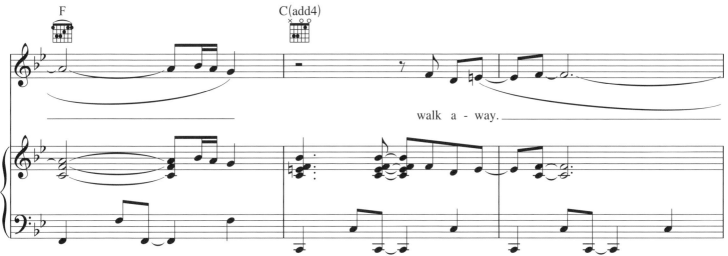

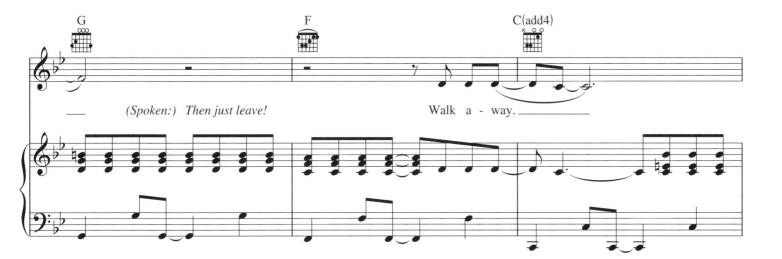

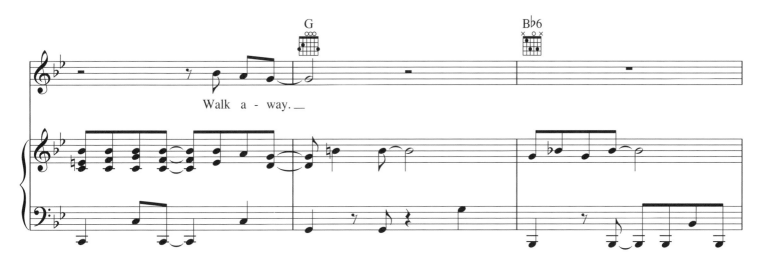

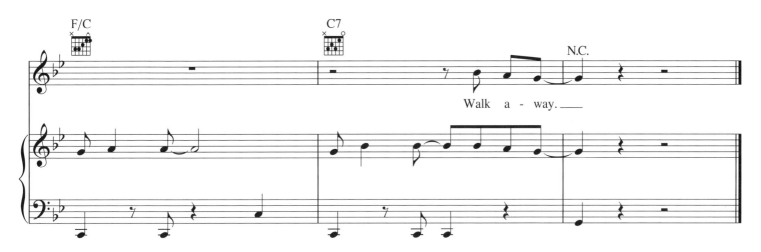

YOU FOUND ME

Words and Music by JOHN SHANKS
and KARA DioGUARDI

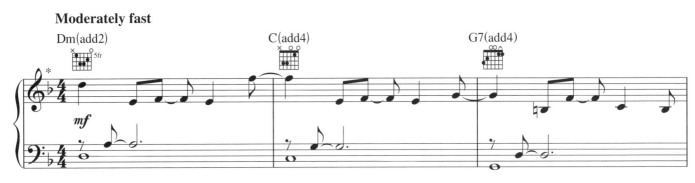

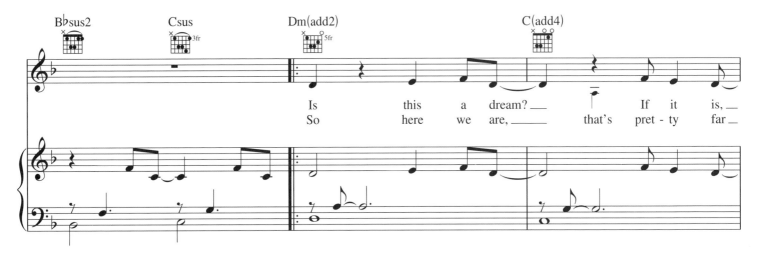

Is this a dream? ___ If it is, ___
So here we are, ___ that's pret-ty far ___

___ please don't wake ___ me from ___ this high. ___
___ when you think ___ me of where ___ we've been. ___

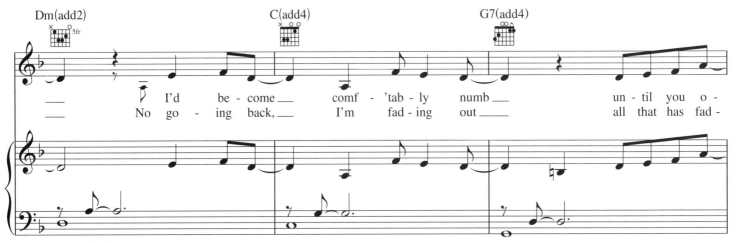

___ I'd be-come ___ comf-'tab-ly numb ___ un-til you o-
___ No go-ing back, ___ I'm fad-ing out ___ all that has fad-

Recorded a half step lower.

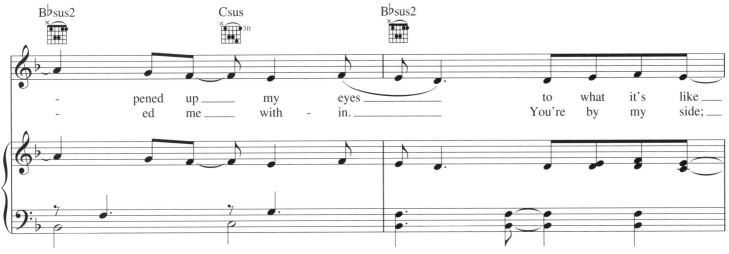

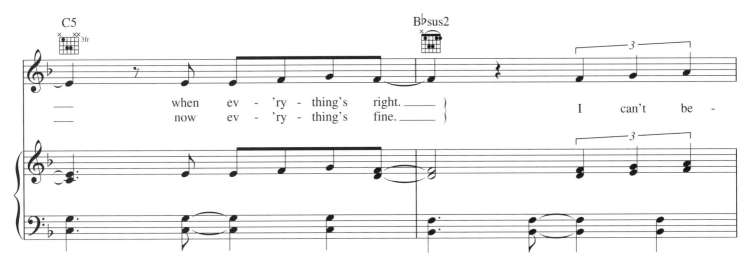

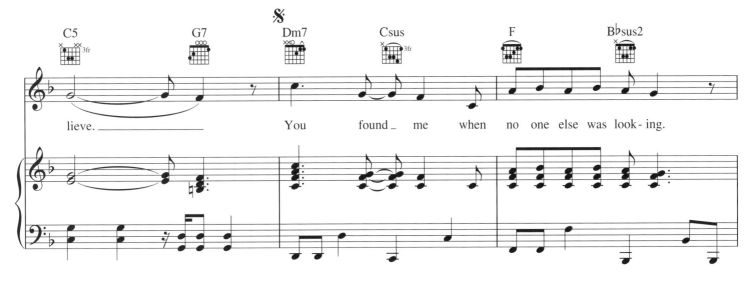

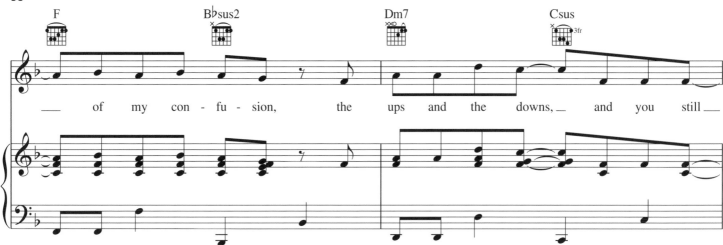

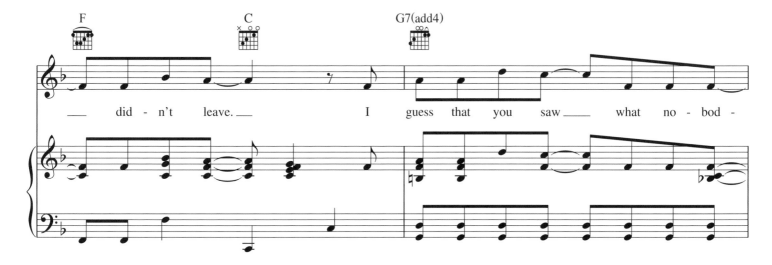

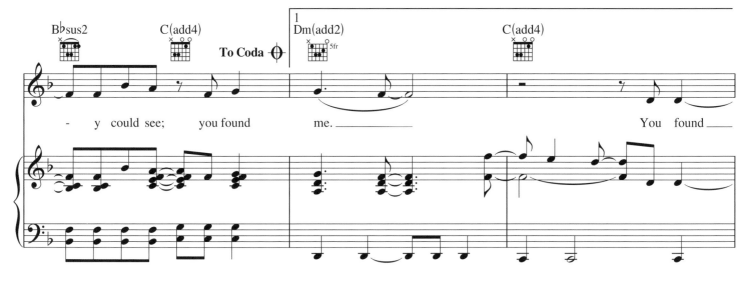

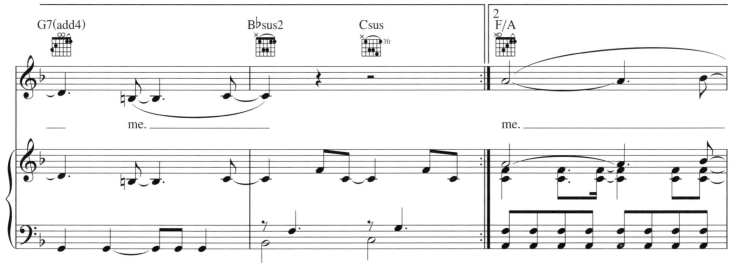

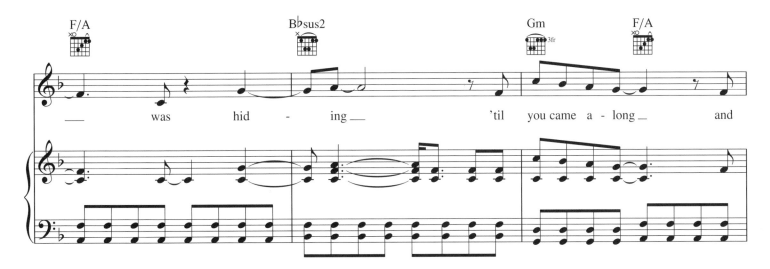

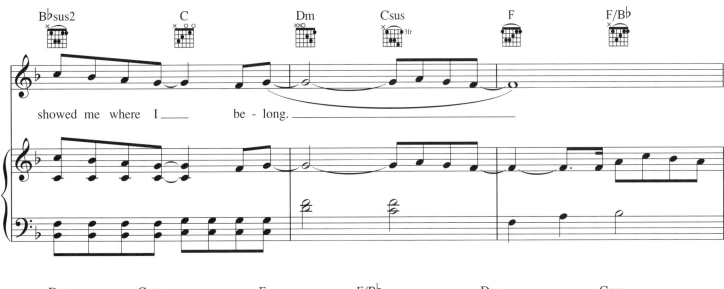

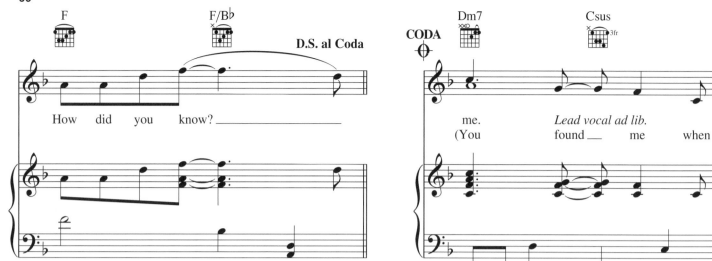

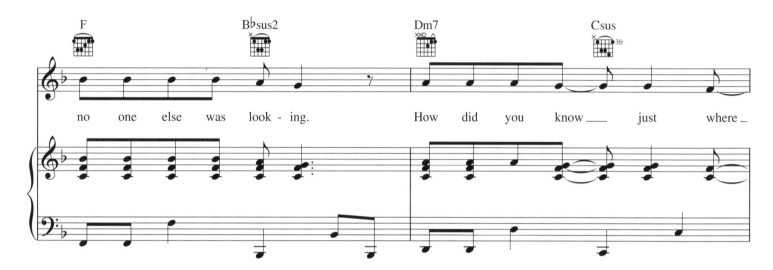

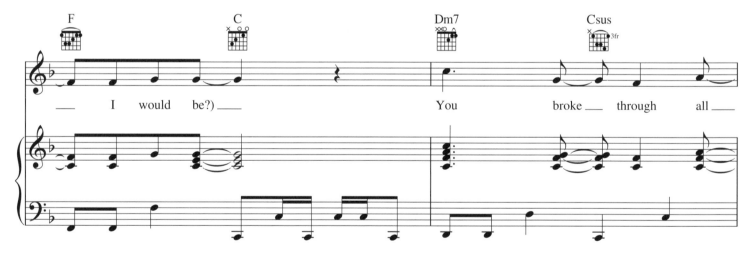

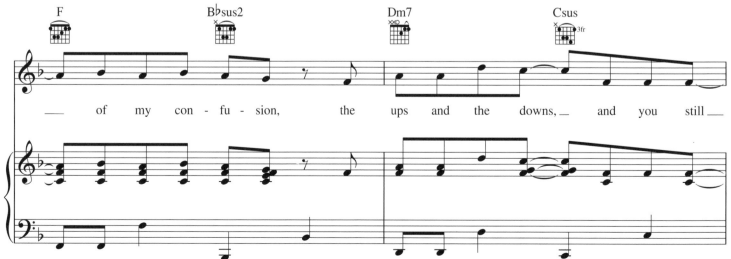

F   C   G7(add4)

_ did - n't leave. _   I guess that you saw _ what no - bod -

B♭sus2   G7(add4)

- y could see; _   the good and the bad _ and the things _

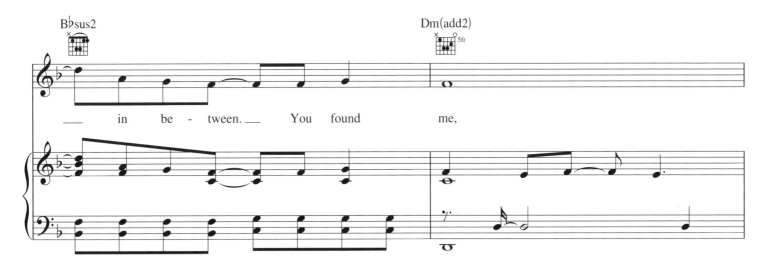

B♭sus2   Dm(add2)

_ in be - tween. _ You found   me,

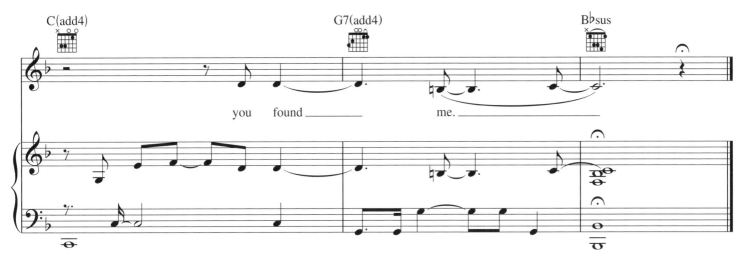

C(add4)   G7(add4)   B♭sus

you found _   me. _____

I HATE MYSELF FOR LOSING YOU

Words and Music by JIMMY HARRY,
SHEPPARD SOLOMON and KARA DioGUARDI

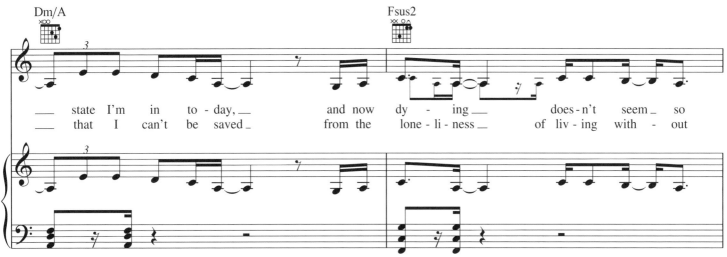

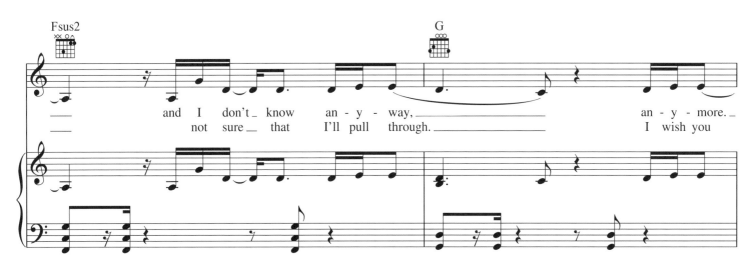

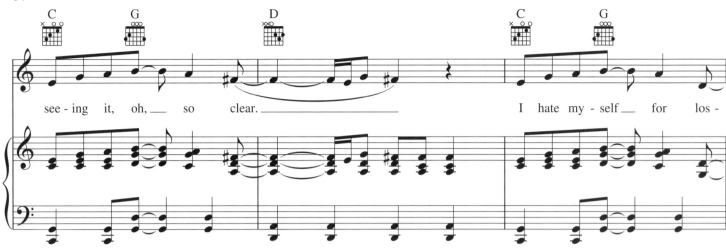

see - ing it, oh,___ so clear._____ I hate my - self___ for los -

- ing you._____ What do you do___ when you look in the mir-ror and

star - ing at you____ is why____ he's not here?_____

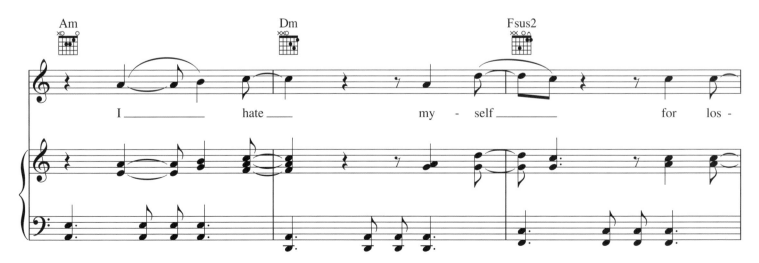

I _____ hate ____ my - self _____ for los -

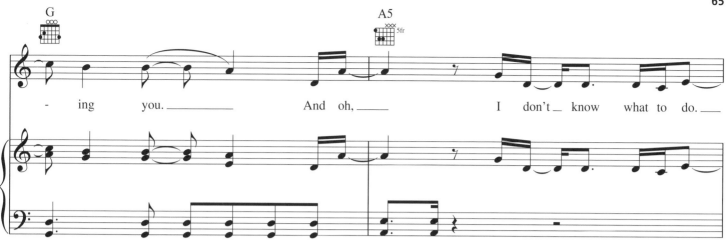

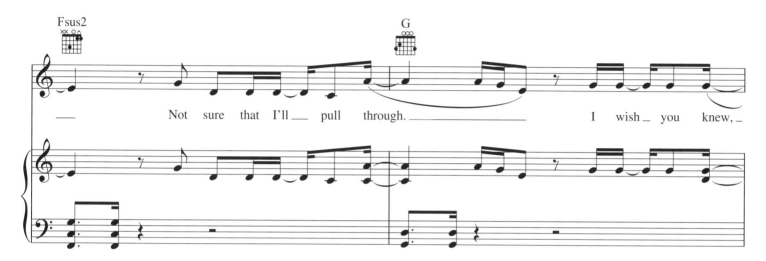

no, _____ no. _____ I hate my-self ___ for los -

- ing you. _____ I'm see-ing it all ___ so, I'm

see-ing it all ___ so clear. _____ I hate my-self ___ for los -

- ing you. _____ What do you do ___ when you look in the mir-ror and

HEAR ME

Words and Music by CLIF MAGNESS,
KELLY CLARKSON and KARA DioGUARDI

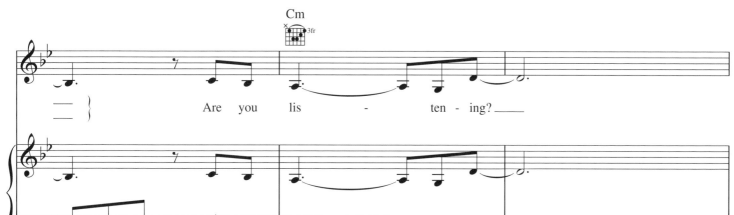

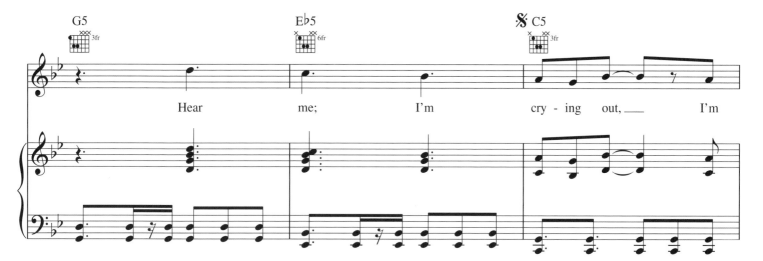

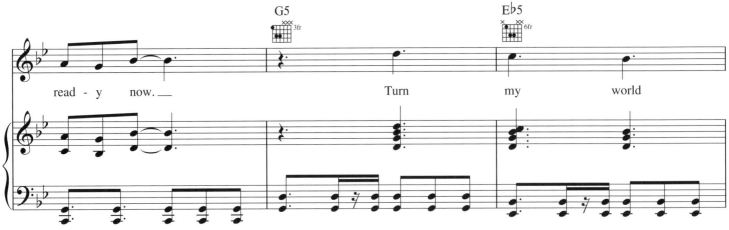

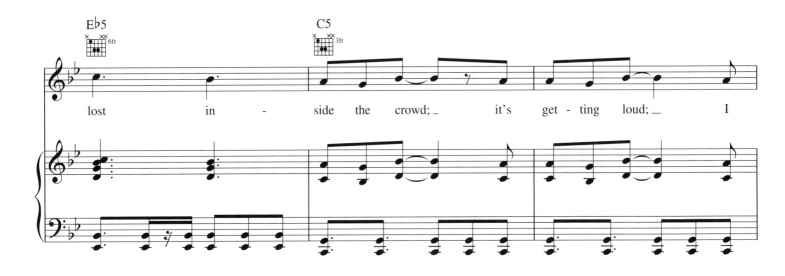

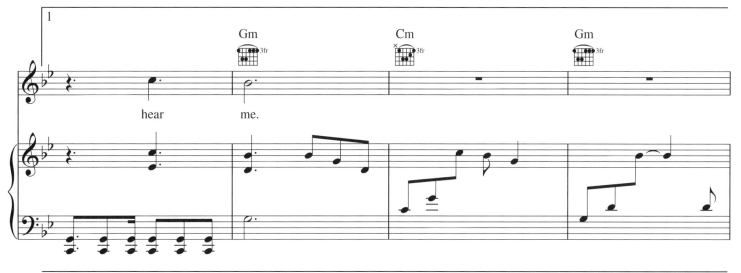

Gm   Cm   Gm

hear   me.

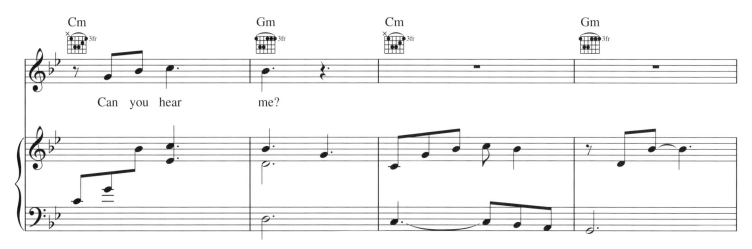

Cm   Gm   Cm   Gm

Can you hear   me?

2

G5

(Hear   me.)   I'm   rest - less and wild, ___   I

Eb5   C5

fall but I try. I need some - one to un - der - stand. ___   I'm
(Can you hear me?)

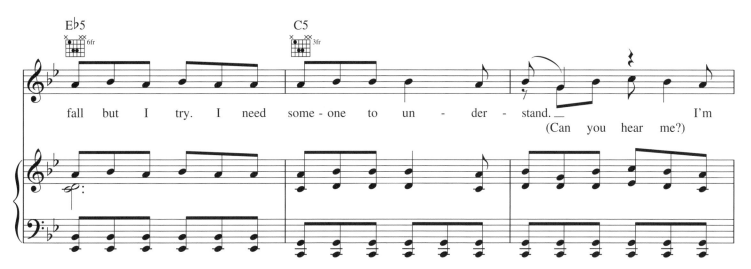

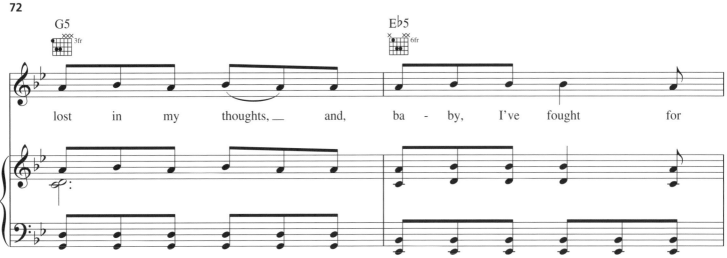

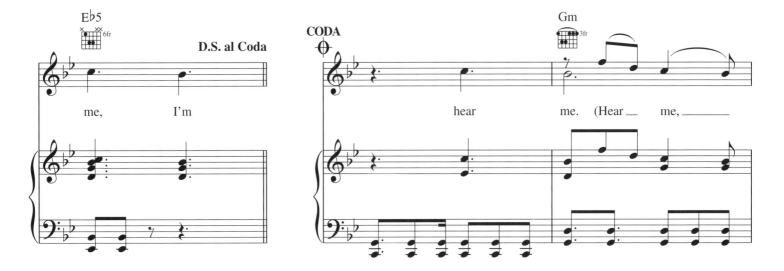

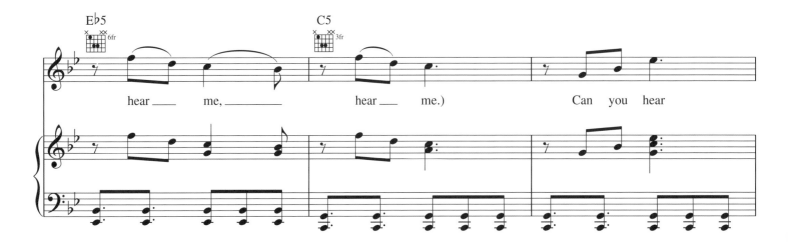

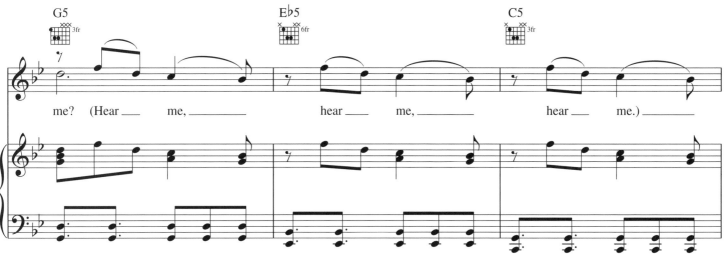

me? (Hear ___ me, _____ hear ___ me, _____ hear ___ me.) _____

Can you hear _____ me?   *Lead vocal ad lib.*

Hear ___ me, ___

hear ___ me, ___   hear ___ me. _____

BEAUTIFUL DISASTER (LIVE)

Words and Music by REBECCA JOHNSON
and MATTHEW WILDER

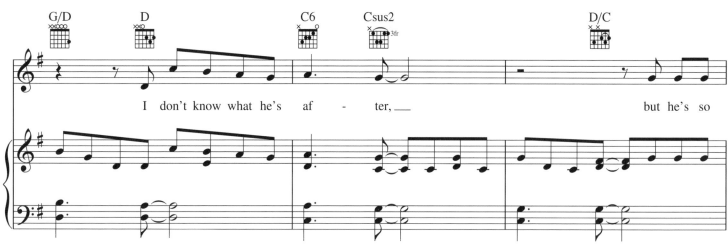

I don't know what he's af - ter, ___ but he's so

beau - ti - ful, he's such a beau-ti-ful dis - as - ter.

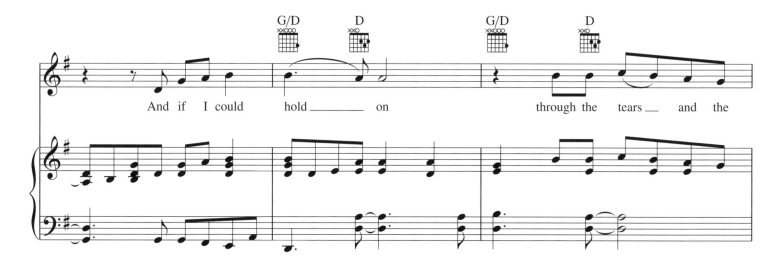

And if I could hold ____ on through the tears ___ and the

laugh - ter, would it be beau - ti - ful,

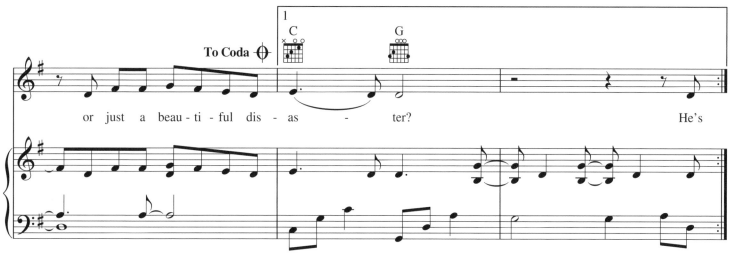

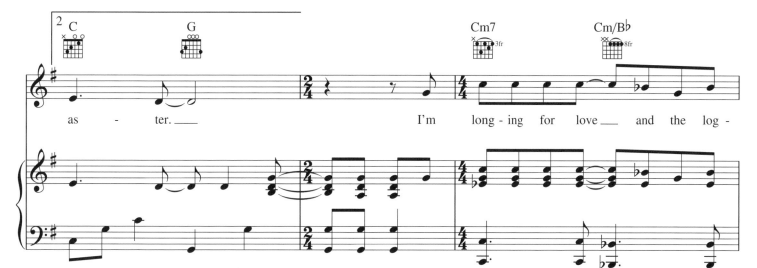

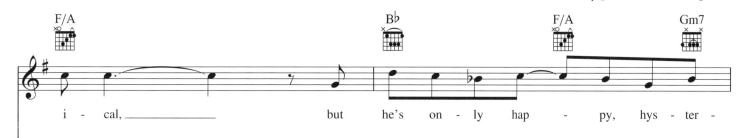

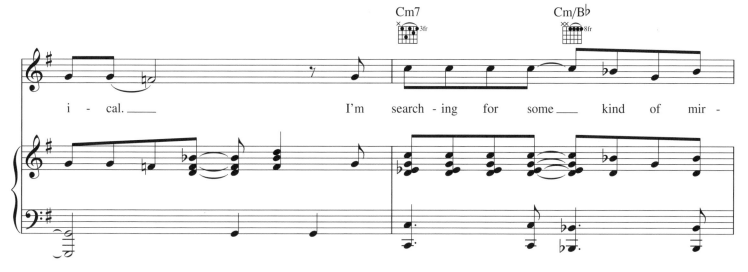

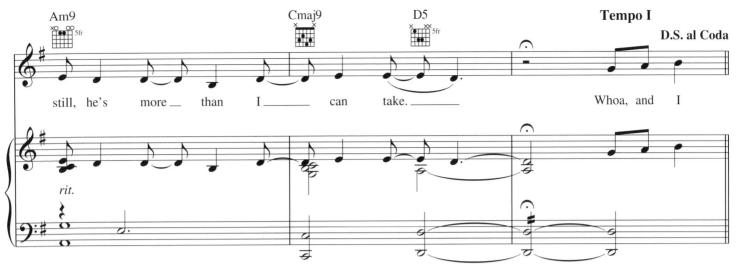

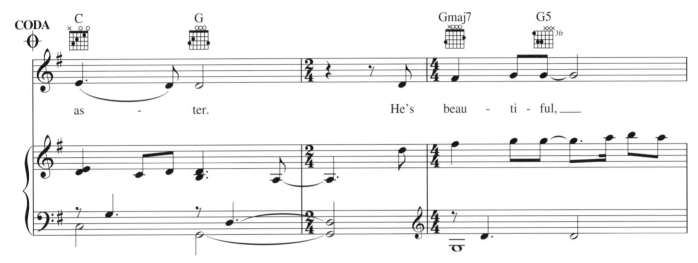

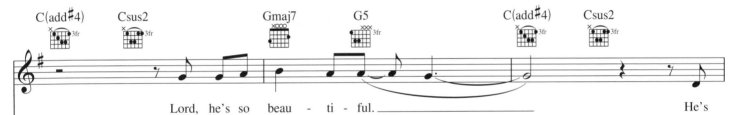

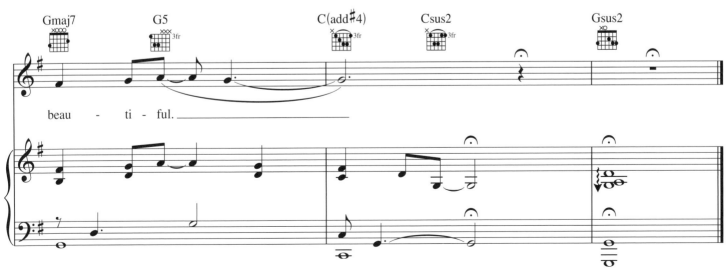